ANIMALS AND THEIR BABIES
Butterflies and Caterpillars

written by Anita Ganeri

illustrated by Anni Axworthy

A Cherrytree book

Published by
Evans Publishing Group
2A Portman Mansions
Chiltern St
London W1U 6NR

First published in 2007

Printed in China by WKT Co Ltd

British Library Cataloguing in Publication Data
Ganeri, Anita, 1961-
   Butterflies and caterpillars. - (Animals and their babies)
   1. Caterpillars - Juvenile literature 2. Butterflies - Life
   cycles - Juvenile literature
   I. Title
   595.7'89156

ISBN 978184 234440 8

CONTENTS

A butterfly starts its life as a tiny egg.
A female butterfly lays the eggs in springtime.
She lays the eggs on plant leaves.

The female only lays one egg at a time but she can lay as many as 100 eggs a day. She lays her eggs, then she flies away.

About a week later, the eggs start to hatch.
Inside each egg is a tiny caterpillar.
The caterpillar chews a hole in its eggshell.

Then the caterpillar wriggles out of the hole.
It is hard work to squeeze all the way out.

The caterpillar is hungry!
It munches on the leaves.
It uses its jaws to bite
off pieces of the leaves.

The caterpillar is growing fast.
Soon its skin gets so tight,
it splits open.

There is a new, bigger
skin underneath.
The growing caterpillar
changes its skin five times.

When it is three weeks old,
the caterpillar is fully grown.
It is ready to turn into a butterfly.
First, it hangs upside down from a leaf.

Then the caterpillar's skin
splits for the last time.
There is a hard case underneath.
This case is called a chrysalis.

Inside the chrysalis, an amazing change takes place. The wriggling little caterpillar turns into...

...a beautiful butterfly!

It takes about 12 days for the butterfly
to grow inside the chrysalis.
Then the chrysalis splits open
and the butterfly
pulls itself out.

At first, the
butterfly's wings
are soft and wet.

It holds them out in the sun
to dry and go hard. Now the
butterfly is ready to fly away.

Butterflies fly about to find food
and places to rest. They also need to
fly away from danger. Hungry birds like
juicy butterflies to eat.

Butterflies eat a sweet juice from inside flowers. The juice is called nectar.

On a sunny, summer's day, you might see butterflies flying from flower to flower.

The butterfly pokes its long tongue inside
a flower. Then it starts to slurp! When it
has finished, it rolls its tongue back up.

Next spring, it is time for a male butterfly to meet a female. This is called mating. After mating, the female butterfly lays her eggs on leaves.

Soon tiny caterpillars will hatch out of the eggs. And the caterpillars will turn into...

...lots of beautiful new butterflies!

Index

Further Information

The butterflies featured in this book are Red Admirals (*Vanessa atlanta*). To find out more about them, you can visit:

www.ukbutterflies.co.uk

www.ladywildlife.com